A BOY AND HIS BIBLE

The Story of Robert Hicks
by Jill Gupta

First published in Great Britain in 2008
by Creative Publishing
Downwood, Claverton Down Road, Bath, Avon BA2 6DT
A C.I.P. catalogue record for this book is available
from the British Library.

Designed by Steve Carroll
Edited by Jill Gupta
Illustrations by Annabelle Hicks
Photographs © Mirrorpix
Printed in China
ISBN 0-7554-7970-X

Prologue

After overseeing and witnessing 10,000 churches and hundreds and thousands of Christians making use of the 8 million commemoration Gospels we produced at the turn of the Millennium, and after working with the 'Daily Telegraph' and other newspapers on Gospel and Bible promotions, I came to some firm convictions concerning the future.

The first is that we needed a 'Welcome Back to Church' initiative. I carried this persuasion around with me and shared it with various individuals and organisations. A BBC Producer for 'Songs of Praise' encouraged me to share my persuasion with the Communications Director of Manchester Diocese, and as they say, "The rest is history".

Alongside 'Welcome Back to Church', I had the persuasion that the first century style and language and of the Gospel text – whether in traditional or modern translations – is itself an obstacle to over 85% of the population today. So I dreamed of the 'Fresh Retelling' of the four Gospels and I am thrilled that Paul Langham, a Cambridge graduate and father of four and the Minister of a large and growing church in Bath, England, undertook to 'retell' the text for contemporary readers. The objective was simple: to draw the reader into the Gospel events as if he were witnessing them. They are meant as a prelude to the reading of the Bible Gospels themselves, as well as an introduction to the heart of the Bible and the subject of the Gospels; Jesus Christ the Son of God.

Today, 'Welcome Back to Church' and the 'Fresh Retelling' of the Gospels make a successful contribution to those churches, church groups and individuals who take them up.

In this autobiography, we have an objective account of the events of my life, in a compact and easy-to-read style. Many of the details are based on my own book, 'A Child Cries' covering my first 15 years, which is of course subjective. I have found it interesting to read about myself in this objective way. I find it difficult to believe that the boy who at the age of 15 could not read, write or speak intelligently, is now the father of 5 children, and 14 grandchildren, who became successful in both retailing and publishing and is still enthusiastic about the Bible, the Gospel and the Essence of both: Jesus Christ the Son of God. It's hard to believe this is true; but God does work in the most unlikely and unexpected ways and I have no doubt I am but one of many who witness God's sovereignity and providence.

What I find more incredible is that this has taken place in spite of the numerous flaws in my makeup as a human being and the multitude of mistakes (which the Bible calls 'sins') that are part and parcel of who I am. Yet the same 'Good Book' makes it clear that "if we confess our sins, the Lord Jesus is faithful and just to forgive us our sins and to cleanse us from all unrighteousness". For this, I am most grateful.

Robert Frederick Hicks, 'The Boy'
Spring 2008, Bath, England

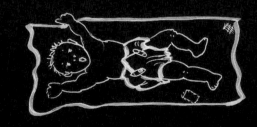

'I like it here. It's warm and there's hot food and children to play with. But it won't last.'

The woman held the little boy firmly by the hand as she marched him along the endless corridors of the Children's Home. It was only a few days to Christmas and she had more than enough to do but she'd been called away from her duties in order to hand four-year-old Robert Hicks over to his mother. Robert was dragging his feet. She gave his hand a little tug and his feet skittered on the highly polished floor. Surely the boy should be glad to be going home to his family instead of being shut up in this huge institution? His mother must have told him it was only a temporary arrangement while she went into a nursing home to have her baby.

7

'I was her fourth child but she never knew my birthday. She never knew me – not even for one day in a year.'

Robert's mother was waiting for her son just inside the doorway of the Infirmary, her six-year- old daughter, Jean, beside her. Although still a young woman, she looked tired and worn. She hardly acknowledged Robert. She did not kiss or hug him but just murmured a brief word of thanks to the member of staff as she signed some papers. Then with a brisk 'Come on' to the little boy she turned on her heel and walked out into the garden surrounding the Home. Robert didn't think to ask about the newborn baby or where his four brothers were. He

had recognised his mother but she was like a stranger to him, a malevolent stranger come to take him away from a place that was safe and warm, where there was plenty of food and space to play games.

From the day he'd been born in February 1941 Robert had known only confusion and uncertainty. Unloved and neglected by his mother he and his brothers and sister alternated between being put in care and living in squalor in the slums of Birmingham. The short time he'd spent in Erdington Cottage Homes had been a taste of Paradise. The adults didn't shout or scream or threaten him. They cared about him and showed they cared. And Christmas was coming. Robert had never experienced Christmas or birthday celebrations. The other children had told him about being given presents and having masses of extra-special food and lots of fun. The little boy's excited anticipation knew no bounds but when he had seen his mother his heart sank. He was being given away to this woman whose very smell made him recoil and even worse, he was going to miss out on Christmas.

No one can see my tears because they're inside, deep inside, and they hurt.

The door swung shut behind them. It was bitterly cold outside. A thick layer of snow carpeted the ground. Robert's mother wore gloves but Jean's only protection was newspaper wrapped round her hands and feet. As Robert trudged along trying to hold back the tears he thrust his hands deep into his pockets in a vain attempt to keep them warm. His

9

pockets were empty and with a sickening start he
realised that, in the hustle and bustle of leaving,
he'd left his treasures behind – a handful of precious
pennies, a bar of Cadbury's chocolate and a hoop-la
game. Robert walked from the big house, past the
magnificent clock tower, down to the tram stop
unconscious of where he was going, unable to think
of anything other than what he was leaving behind.
He trailed behind his mother and sister breaking
into a trot in response to his mother's constant
demands that he keep up. At last they reached the
tram stop and boarded a tram. All the downstairs
seats were taken so they climbed to the top and sat
on wooden benches in the open. Robert sat on his
own behind his mother and Jean. The spark of
excitement he'd experienced when he got on the
tram and it moved off (for he had never travelled on
one before) was soon snuffed out by the cold and his
misery.

When they reached Birmingham city centre they
changed on to a bus. The Christmas lights were
dazzling but Robert felt uncomfortable in this vast
alien world. He longed for familiar sights and sounds
but everything was strange. It was not surprising
that he didn't recognise anything for his mother was
taking him to a new home. His family was one of
the many chosen by the council to be re-housed in
the countryside outside Birmingham now the war
was over.

Robert sat upstairs staring out through the dirty
windows while Jean and his mother stayed downstairs.

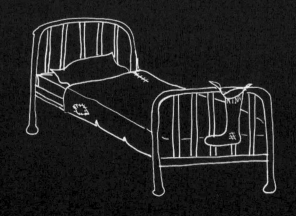

The journey took about forty minutes and all the time Robert was uncomfortably conscious of being transported somewhere from which there would be no escape.

When they got off the bus and walked to their new home in Bartley Green it wasn't the sight of the house that struck Robert but the silence and the absence of the nauseating smells of the slums. Fields surrounded the terraced houses and it was so quiet Robert could hear their every step.

A neighbour had lit a fire in one room of the Hicks' new home. The rest of the house was icily cold. It smelt of the emulsion paint the local council had slapped on in an effort to make the place look clean. Robert was packed off to bed immediately. He was hungry and cold but his mother didn't offer him any food or a hot drink so he slipped miserably between grubby sheets in a bed already occupied by his two younger brothers, Bernard and Brian.

I think I should be happy. Something must be wrong.

By Christmas the whole family was installed in 335 Stonehouse Lane apart from William Hicks, the head of the household who was serving in the army, but was soon to be demobbed. Robert still felt resentful. His mother had done nothing to prepare the house for her young family. There was no food in the larder. There was no proper bedding and not a single paper chain or sprig of holly as a token of Christmas. Robert longed with all his heart to be

13

back in the Children's Home. He was too young to realize that his mother's Army Allowance was drastically reduced when he and his siblings were in care and that she missed out on Family Allowance and the coupons in the children's ration books. Despite money being tight other people noticed that Mrs Hicks had chocolates, cigarettes, stockings and money for other luxuries and they drew their own conclusions. Getting her children back certainly boosted her income and enabled her to buy more clothes and food. As for the newborn baby – she had been put up for adoption.

Robert spent Christmas Eve with his younger brothers and sister while their mother went back to the city to collect their elder brothers, Donald and John, from the Homes. Before she left Robert begged her to bring back his shiny pennies, bar of chocolate and hoop-la game but when, eventually, they returned she only gave him the game. His brothers had eaten the chocolate and Donald said he couldn't find the pennies. Robert fought back the tears of disappointment. He had learned from an early age that crying got you nowhere in the Hicks family. He was sure that Donald had kept the money for himself but what really riled him was that his brothers had not even saved him a single square of chocolate.

I feel so cold and hungry and I don't think Christmas is going to come to our house

Christmas Day dawned and Robert woke to find stockings on the bed. He and his brothers opened them eagerly. They each had an apple, an orange

"The perfect FRIEND is one who knows
the best and worst of us
and loves us just the same."

and a few boiled sweets but the stockings mostly contained balls of crumpled paper. December 25th 1946 was the only time Robert was given a stocking. There were no Christmas presents for him, Donald, Bernard or Brian. John and Jean were more fortunate. John was given a fountain pen with ink and a note-book. He treasured this gift and Jean's second-hand doll's house and set of miniature kitchen furniture became very special to her. Everyone else went without apart from Mrs Hicks who treated herself to a new dress, overcoat and shoes.

Christmas dinner was no more than bread and a scrape of lard. Robert ate it without tasting a single mouthful. He could not stop thinking about what Christmas day would have been like if his mother hadn't collected him from the Homes. He stared at the small, framed text which a previous tenant had left hanging on the wall. It read: 'The Perfect Friend is one who knows the best and worst of us and loves us just the same'. Robert repeated the words over and over again in his head. They seemed to be mocking him yet he longed for them to be true.

The house was cold, dark and gloomy, lit only by gas and since there was nothing else to eat Robert decided to explore outside. He wrapped newspaper around his feet and ventured out into the snow. A weak winter sun lit up a landscape which made the little boy gasp with wonder. Trees, fields and hedges wore a sparkling mantle of pure white and to Robert's young eyes the countryside spread out before him looked like fairyland.

As the weather deteriorated, becoming even more bitterly cold, the children were forced to stay indoors. They had nothing to do other than playing with Robert's hoop-la game. It was a depressing time for all of them and the feeling that he was a stranger within his own family compounded Robert's misery. He had no one to talk to about his worries and fears so he bottled them up inside him. At the same time he was already aware that he didn't speak properly so anyone other than his parents and siblings found it difficult to understand him.

Unable to articulate his thoughts and with no one to whom he could express his emotions Robert felt frustrated and ignored. He endured that first winter in Bartley Green feeling isolated and unwanted. At last spring came and the children were able to get out of the house. Robert loved exploring the fields and at first he tried to join in the gangs of local children. Before long, though, he found himself alone again as his older brothers went off with their own age group and Bernard and Brian joined Jean's gang. There was something to look forward too, though – father was coming home.

Mom and Dad don't notice me. I speak but no one listens.

Convinced that their Dad was a hero, the children waited for his return with impatient excitement. When he arrived he looked just as they had imagined he would – dressed in a thick army overcoat with shining buttons and with a highly polished army

19

issue leather belt holding up the trousers of his demob suit. He came with a friend who intended to stay for a couple of days but the children hardly noticed his pal for their father took centre stage and gloried in the attention he received.

For a few short hours Robert was proud of his Dad and enjoyed listening to his tales of what he had done in the war – stories in which William Hicks displayed courage and daring beyond the call of duty. As all the children hung on their father's every word that night, Robert felt part of the family for a brief moment, no longer an outsider, but this 'happy family' experience was as false as it was fleeting. With father back life at 335 was about to change dramatically. It had been a cold, hungry and miserable existence. It became Hell on earth.

21

I keep humming quietly to myself. I don't know why, but the vibration from the humming stops the pain from thoughts I cannot share with anyone.

Robert wandered through the fields humming and occasionally talking to himself. It became a habit that lasted a decade and it got on everyone's nerves. But Robert found it relaxing and calming. He loved being in the countryside. He gloried in the fresh air, the space, and the sound of bird song. It was such a contrast to the filthy, cobbled courtyards of the slums where he used to play. Outdoors Robert felt free. He walked and ran, jumped across streams, rode the farmers' horses bareback and attempted to catch frogs and fish. Most of all he tried to forget that he would have to return to 335 Stonehouse Lane.

Back indoors Robert would sink silently into himself. His mother ignored him, as she did all her offspring. His father ruled the household through fear and the threat of a beating with the leather army belt.

I don't want to come home until it is dark, because then I can crawl into bed without Mom or Dad knowing. I don't think they miss me anyway.

When William Hicks got a job at a local factory he didn't spend his wages on the children who were in desperate need of new clothes but on going to the pub and the cinema with his wife. They were both perfectly happy to leave the children at home to look after themselves. For a few short hours the tension in the house relaxed but once the adults returned the arguments started, often escalating into violent rows. Robert lay in the bed he shared with his brothers clutching the thin sheet, their only covering, close to him and trying to block out the sound of angry voices. Two topics always led to trouble – the baby Robert's mother had had adopted and her infidelity.

23

I like Miss Treadwell. When she looks at me she smiles at me. Mom never looks at me or smiles.

School offered some relief from the misery of life at home. Miss Treadwell, the headmistress of the village school, never lost her temper. Robert thought the world of her and she made sure he was given an extra bottle of milk whenever possible. He was always hungry so school diners were an important part of Robert's day but they came at a cost. As he

lined up week by week to hand the teacher the coupons entitling him to free meals Robert would feel his face going red. He would stare at the floor hoping no one would notice he was flushed with shame. He felt the same when he had to go to the NSPCC to be kitted out with 'new' second-hand clothes. Being labelled 'the poorest of the poor' was hard to live with and Robert was only too aware that the better off children looked down on him and his family. He hated the humiliation of free school meals but at least he was able to enjoy the generous servings of hot food dished out by dinner ladies who recognized how much he needed a decent meal. But what Robert needed more than anything was love and attention. There were no hugs and kisses at home. His mother didn't want him anywhere near her. Robert struggled to understand why. What was wrong with him? What had he done to make her ignore his very existence? He knew she was unhappy out in the country and longed to return to city life. She made a start by going back to her old factory job and was soon working six days a week and scarcely seeing her children. She spent her wages on new clothes for herself while they wore cast-offs. But the more she worked the worse the rows became. One Sunday the violence got out of hand. Robert cowered in a corner, his hands pressed tightly over his ears as he tried to block out the screams punctuated by angry accusations. His father was beside himself with rage and frightened for her life, Robert's mother shouted at him to call the police. Robert ran out of the house as fast as his legs would carry him. Panting with panicky fear he reached the public phone box outside the village store and dialled 999. He was too scared

25

to go back into the house but the fight was over by the time the police arrived. Robert's father never forgave him for calling the police and beat him time and again for grassing him up.

Why can't we just be normal the same as everybody else?

As the years passed Robert's mum came home from work later and later sometimes staying away for the whole night. She always had an excuse but her husband was suspicious. He would drag the children out of bed, line them up in the kitchen and, belt in hand, interrogate them as to their mother's whereabouts and behaviour. Number 335 was not a home but a place of fear and suffering. Donald took most of the beatings. John had asthma so badly that he often had to go into hospital. Jean and Bernard both had eye problems and Robert was tongue-tied. Nothing was done about the children's health. The adults in the family were only interested in themselves.

Slowly I'm losing my family. It's like a slow death.

Robert was ten when his mother fell pregnant. She was having an affair with a West Indian man who worked at her factory. Once she was pregnant there was no turning back. She made a decision that was to have dire consequences for her children. She walked out on them, leaving them in the 'care' of a violent and unstable man, and never made contact again for twenty-eight long years.

27

On 9 June 1952 the Hicks children were abandoned by their mother and left to the mercy of their cruel bully of a father. Robert couldn't believe that his mother was really going. He was stunned and bewildered. John refused to accept what was happening. When he saw his mother board the bus for Birmingham he ran after her. The bus pulled away but still he chased after it desperately hoping that she would change her mind. The bus disappeared from view leaving John broken hearted and struggling for breath.

Jean was so frightened by the prospect of what might happen when her father came home that night that she ran away. She slept under the hedgerows and when the police finally picked her up she refused to go back to 335 and went to live with relations for the next two years. Soon after Jean left, Bernard and Brian were sent to a children's home, John went into a convalescent home and Robert was packed off to Middlemore Homes, an institution for orphaned and neglected children.

Robert was lost and confused. He missed his brothers and sister and the strict discipline and regimentation at the Homes did nothing to ease his misery. He felt deserted and alone, unwanted and worthless. Six months later he was told he was going home. Robert was scared and he had good reason to be. His father's behaviour had deteriorated since his wife had left him and Robert was going to be there alone with him. He would be the butt of all his father's rages, the sole victim of his vicious interrogations. With no one to turn to for help Robert decided that he must do everything possible to avoid confrontation. Once

back at 335 he kept the house spotless. He polished
and dusted, washed and ironed, went without food,
did whatever he could to prevent his father finding
an excuse for losing his temper and laying into him.

*My Mom has gone. My family has gone. I am all
alone again.*

Alone, purposeless, convinced that nobody loved
him and suspicious of all adults, Robert dragged
himself through each joyless day. His brothers came
home but not for long. Brian ran away and was sent
to a boys' institution when the police caught up with
him. Donald had got into trouble and was sent to a
reform school. Bernard, like John, had to go into a
convalescent home because his asthma worsened
after his mother left. For months at a time Robert
was on his own with his father. Now a teenager, he
was able to get a few odd jobs and used the money
he earned to go the cinema and escape into a world
of fantasy and adventure. He too tried running away
only to be stopped and questioned by a policeman
twenty-four hours later and escorted back to his
father and to a whack across his head.

*When I grow up, I will never cry again because when
I'm an adult no one will be able to hurt me.*

Although Robert pleaded with his father to stop
hurting him the physical, mental and emotional
torment carried on. William Hicks seemed to get
some sort of perverse satisfaction in persecuting his
son but worse was to happen when Jean came home

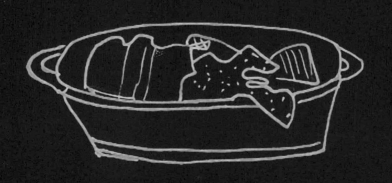

after two years in Sheffield and a spell in Erdington Cottage Homes. By this time Brian was back home, and John returned for brief spells. Betty, a friend of their father's had moved in. None of the children realized that she was a prostitute and they were grateful for the small kindnesses she showed them. When William Hicks was sent down for forty-two days for not paying Jean's keep while she was away Betty was left in sole charge of the children. As soon as he was locked up, Betty started bringing clients back to the house, and then one evening she took Jean, who was in her early teens, off to Birmingham and abandoned her in the city late at night. Jean got home safely but Betty was never seen again. The children were put into care once more until their father was released from prison. The experience had not changed him. Jean took over the cleaning, cooking and ironing. She was terrified of her father and devastated by her mother's desertion. One night her father came home late. He was drunk. Jean got up to cook him a meal. Afterwards in the dark he raped her. He threatened to kill Jean if she told anyone so Jean kept silent. Robert noticed that the bullying eased up and was grateful for it but he had no idea that his father was abusing his sister. Jean became deeply depressed. She concocted a plan to murder her father and asked her brothers to help her. They were more than willing to do so but at the last minute they held back from gassing their father while he slept. The violence got worse. Brian was brutally beaten with a brass fender leaving him battered and bruised. Robert was petrified that he was going to be subjected to the same treatment. But that day he made a resolution. He was going to

33

stand up to his father. If he had to, he would fight him rather than submit to the terrible suffering he'd inflicted on the youngest member of the family.

I am afraid that someone's going to get killed.

Fear was turning into hatred. Robert hated his father for not loving him; for caring only about himself; for being a hypocrite; for being a useless father; for not being bothered about whether his son existed or not. As he grew older Robert became even more aware of his lost childhood and he grieved for it. He was nearly fifteen and he had known only pain and humiliation, desertion and hardship. He could not speak clearly, organize his thoughts or read and write adequately. His only refuge was a corner in a downstairs room where he copied out words from comics. Robert wanted to escape but he also wanted to take control of his life. Brian's battered leg had forced him to think about standing up to his father and when his headmaster told him he was a failure, Robert became even more determined to change his life.

One night he was alone in the house. He had spent the evening in his corner working by candlelight once the gas ran out. He went to bed still wearing his socks and shirt ready for when his father returned home and called him down to make him a sandwich. The shirt was a cheap nylon one his dad had got from a man in a pub. He'd given it to Robert – the only gift he ever gave him. It was gone midnight when Robert heard the door bang. He pictured his father in the kitchen feeding the meter then lighting the gas oven and warming himself by its heat. The

35

call came soon enough and Robert quickly put on his trousers and shoes and ran down the bare wooden stairs. His father wanted tea and Robert made it and poured it into two jam jars. The only two cups in the house were for visitors only.

I have to face my deepest fear ... I have to face Dad.

William Hicks soon started ranting about his wife and that led him to recall the time Robert had called the police. His eyes glazed over, his body started to twitch and Robert knew that he was about to lash out. As his father lurched towards him he screwed up his courage and punched him in the stomach with every ounce of strength his body possessed. His dad doubled over and, for an instant, father and son looked into one another's eyes. Robert saw fear and the hatred within him melted away but he was still in danger so he jerked his knee up catching his father full on the jaw. Blood spurted across Robert's shirt and trickled down it, vivid red against the yellow nylon. There was a knife nearby and a pan of hot water on the stove but Robert didn't need to inflict further damage on his father. He was no longer frightened of the man who lay in a heap on the floor. When Robert went to bed that night he was conscious that he had changed. He felt calm and confident because he was never going to let anyone bully or beat him again. Robert had broken free from his father but his next challenge was to escape from the confines of his trapped mind and speech impediment.

37

I am now a grown up boy, but what shall I do with my life?

Robert left school when he was fifteen. He couldn't read or write properly, the soles of his shoes were tied to the uppers with string and the pressure was on from his father who couldn't wait to help himself to Robert's wages. Despite all the obstacles in his way Robert managed landed the job of errand boy with a local branch of 'George Mason – The Family Grocer'. He got a bike to go with the job and a weekly wage of two pounds eighty! Robert felt a little flush of pride and satisfaction when he picked up his first pay packet. He'd worked for it and his work had been valued. He could see the first glimmerings of a future in which he'd move forward, learn new things and earn enough money to be totally independent. His father brought him down to earth in his usual cruel and selfish way. He snatched Robert's pay slip from him, then took all but five pence of his earnings. Each week Robert was left with five pence to buy clothes, shoes and his lunch. Unsurprisingly Robert didn't tell him that after the first week his wages went up by twenty-five pence!

At home Robert was ignored as his father went out drinking and gambling night after night. At work no one took any notice of the new and most junior member of staff apart from Mrs Siddall, who was training to become a manageress. She was a divorced nurse with teenage children of her own and her heart went out to the young errand boy who was obviously struggling with tremendous problems. She promised to help him and during every lunch break she sat down with him and encouraged him to spell simple words. Robert tried hard but he became frustrated when he failed. He didn't know he was dyslexic, he

just thought he was stupid. Mrs Siddall's attempts to help him pronounce his words more clearly were also doomed to failure but she admired Robert for his persistence and she refused to give up on him. It occurred to her that there might be a physical reason for Robert's difficulties. She took Robert over to a corner of the room and asked him to open his mouth wide. Blushing with embarrassment Robert did as requested and he let her look carefully at the inside of his mouth. She saw immediately that he was tongue-tied. She asked Robert to sit down and described to him what she'd seen and explained that this was the cause of his difficulty in expressing himself. When she told him that it wasn't his fault that he couldn't speak properly Robert felt as if a huge burden had been lifted from his shoulders. Mrs Siddall's excitement was infectious. She said that a simple operation could put things right and Robert promised to go to the doctor's that same night after work. With his heart racing with anticipation Robert went to his GP and two weeks later he presented himself at Selly Oak Hospital for an operation under local anaesthetic.

What do I want ... to be able to talk, to be able to write, to be able to read, to be able to belong, to be able to laugh and to be happy on the inside.

The long, impersonal corridors reminded Robert of the children's homes he been in. Had he not taken down directions on the back of an envelope he would have been hopelessly lost. As it was he arrived at the right clinic in good time. The sister who called him in for his operation was surprised that no one had come with Robert, but he was only too used to being

on his own and at least the surgeon was kind and sensitive. He asked Robert if he would allow a number of students to observe, as it was highly unusual for someone of his age to have such an operation. His problem should have been dealt with in childhood. Robert reluctantly agreed. Knowing now that he had lived all these years with a condition that should have been put right when he was a child shocked and saddened him. It was just another example of his parents' lack of care.

By the time Robert returned to the hospital for his check-up with the surgeon his speech had already improved substantially but he still needed speech therapy which was not available then on the NHS. Although Robert was prepared to save up Mr Hall, his boss, would not allow him to take time off work so he had to forgo the speech therapy. He was able, though, to follow one piece of advice his surgeon had given him after the operation – to copy words out by hand and pronounce each word out loud as he copied it.

Without a book my dreams would crumble ...
I would forever be a worthless nobody.

Robert couldn't wait to get started. He was going to find a book and copy it out page by page. Back at 335 he searched for a book, any book. He tried Jean's room first knowing how much she enjoyed reading but there was not a single book to be found. The boys' bedroom, where sometimes all five of them had to share one bed, was similarly bereft of reading material and since Robert's father only ever read 'The Daily Mirror' there was no point in looking in

his room – a room Robert was reluctant to enter in any case.

Robert began to feel panicky. Finding a book at home had become absolutely vital. The surgeon had said that being tongue-tied had had a negative effect on his self-confidence and his motivation. Robert wasn't tongue-tied any more. He was in control. The future was in his hands. All he needed was a book so he could make a start. Without a book his dreams would crumble and he would be stuck in his old familiar, harsh, grey world where he was a worthless nobody.

Downstairs now, Robert steeled himself to search the cupboard where his father kept his army belt. The cupboard was full of rubbish but Robert explored every inch of it and his persistence was rewarded for there, tucked away in one corner was a book, its cover thick with dust. Robert carried it into the kitchen and wiped the dust and cobwebs from the soft cover. The book's leather binding was now clean but it was decidedly grey and patchy. Robert wanted the book to match up to the huge challenge he was setting himself. He found an old tin of black boot polish, melted some of it down and rubbed it into the leather cover by hand until it was restored to its original glossy black. At last he had a book that looked good enough to play its part in changing his life. He had no idea how radical and far-reaching that change would be!

Mrs Siddall was as keen to help as ever. She gave Robert a large can of ink – enough to fill a hundred bottles! Robert had a pen, now he had ink and all

45

that he required before he started his momentous
task was lots of paper! Desperate to start copying
out all 1400 pages of the book he'd found, Robert
concentrated his energies on finding a free supply
of paper for he had no money to buy any. Work
provided the answer to his problem. From time to
time an outside agency sent a man to Mason's to
check on what stock had been sold. Robert was always
detailed to help the stock taker. When he next came
to the shop Robert went to offer his help but he
couldn't take his eyes off the sheaf of computer sheets
the man was using. He noticed he was writing copious
notes on the back of large printed sheets which were
folded over concertina fashion offering him almost
endless supplies of fresh writing space. Slightly flushed
with embarrassment Robert decided to throw caution
to the wind. Although he didn't really know this
efficient, well-spoken man and, as a young errand
boy, was in awe of him, he blurted out the truth. He
told him how much he wanted to copy out the book
he'd found and how he wished that he had as much
paper at his disposal as the stock taker did. The man
smiled. He didn't dismiss the teenager who'd gone
red with embarrassment or laugh at his intentions.
He didn't question him or undermine his resolve.
Instead he gave him exactly what he needed just
as Mrs Siddall had and in as great a quantity as she.
He told Robert that the sheets he was using were
effectively waste paper and that Robert could have as
many as he wanted. Robert asked for one thousand
four hundred sheets and the next day they were
delivered to him at the shop. That night Robert put
a great wad of paper in the basket of his delivery
bike and cycled home. Exhilaration and excitement

made his heart beat more quickly and he pushed the pedals round as fast as he could. He couldn't wait to get back to 335 and make a start on his great undertaking – to copy every word in the book he'd found – an Authorized Version of the Bible.

Robert started at Genesis chapter one. When he first picked up his pen a great feeling of inspiration and anticipation surged through him but it quickly drained away leaving him frustrated and angry. His writing was too big. There were too many mistakes. He tore off page after page of computer paper, screwed them up and threw them to the floor. Robert knew how he wanted his copy to look so he didn't give up. He concentrated hard and strained every nerve and muscle determined to keep his writing small and neat whilst avoiding errors. It didn't happen immediately but his writing did improve and the number of copied sheets he considered acceptable began to grow. It was a struggle but Robert was winning.

Night after night Robert came home from work, ate quickly then settled himself down with Bible, pen, ink and paper. Tiredness fell away from him as soon as he picked up his pen. He felt a fresh rush of energy and he actually looked forward to the prospect of making progress with the task he'd set himself. He didn't care about sitting all evening facing a brick wall. He was so immersed in copying the Bible page by page that he scarcely ever looked up and if he did he noticed nothing of his surroundings because his mind was fixed on what he'd written and read out loud. Robert was totally committed to the task and his vision and determination never faltered. When

he came to the end of the first ream of paper Robert was overwhelmed by what he had achieved. He stared transfixed by the pile of neatly written sheets of paper – he had done this – this vast amount of careful, painstaking writing was all his own work representing countless hours of solitary dedication evening after evening. He knew how much he had left to do – the scale of the task still remaining was immense but it didn't deter him. It just made him even more determined to see it through.

By the time he had finished copying out Exodus Robert decided to start on the New Testament whilst continuing with The Old Testament. He didn't understand much of what he was writing and pronouncing out loud but it was effecting a change in him. Stimulated intellectually, he felt sharper and better able to express himself. His speech improved and some of the portions of scripture struck a cord with him helping him to understand more about himself. When he copied the words 'the earth was without form and void' from the story of the creation they spoke directly to Robert. He thought about his life and how so much of it had been 'without form and void'. There'd been no love, care or structure. He'd gone from slums to children's homes to 335 and back to institutions. His mother and father had come and gone during his short lifetime, as had his brothers and sister. There had been nothing constant and secure to hang on to until now for at last he was not only moving forward with a purpose but was daring to hope that, as God shaped and developed the earth and all living creatures, he too could become a new creation. Copying the Bible was not a mechanical

exercise for Robert. Once he had conquered the initial problems regarding his handwriting and accuracy he was able to concentrate on what he was copying. Very often Robert would puzzle over the meaning of a passage he'd copied. He would sit, pen in hand, while he tried to would reason it out and then to relate what the passage said to his own life. Jesus' teaching about a way of living based on love, inclusiveness and a personal relationship with God really made an impact on him. Robert had no knowledge of theology but he realized that Jesus was different from every other person in the Bible. As he continued to copy out the Bible it became an integral part of his life and the instrument by which his life was transformed.

I could see a future for myself, a chance to make up for lost time.

Robert was delighted to find that, as his speech improved so did his ability to communicate with others. Within two or three months he was able to hold intelligible conversations with Mrs Siddall. She never stopped encouraging him and the more he talked the more confident Robert grew. His boss soon discovered that Robert had plenty to say for himself. Every night Robert stayed behind to clear up the shop and he used that opportunity to talk to Mr Hall who was waiting to secure the premises.

One day Mr Weston, the regional director, summoned Robert to his office. Robert went, not in fear and trembling because he knew he'd done nothing wrong and now, six months after his operation, he felt

confident enough to speak up for himself. Mr Weston boosted Robert's self-confidence by congratulating him on his standard of work and then offering him an apprenticeship. Robert had dreamed of this but it had seemed no more than that – a pipe dream that would never come true. He was so excited by the prospect of an apprenticeship that he wanted to accept straight away but there was a sting in the tail. If he did decide to become an apprentice he would have to take a pay cut. Robert knew the value of money only too well. He had lived in poverty, gone without food, proper clothing, toys and books. Every penny he'd ever spent had first been earned the hard way. To take a pay cut was a serious choice but Robert was shrewd and forward thinking. An apprenticeship would give him a future and a way to make up for his lost education. He was desperately keen to learn as much as he could. He ached to be successful so he didn't have to think too long about his reply. He chose to be apprenticed with a glad and grateful heart. That evening when he got home Robert laid out paper, pen and ink and opened the Bible. Winning an apprenticeship gave an added impetus to the task and he embraced the challenge of copying out hundreds more pages with the same eagerness and anticipation he had for starting the new chapter in his business life. Even when he found he was copying out long lists of strange names usually prefaced by the word 'begat', Robert persevered. He was thrilled by the changes he recognized in himself and which were apparent to all who knew him. For years he'd had to hold silent conversations with himself but no more. Now he had the confidence and ability to talk to anyone and everyone.

55

For the next three years Robert trained hard. He learnt everything from wholesale buying to display, from accountancy to distribution as well as a vast range of practical skills. It was as if new worlds were being opened up to him and he couldn't learn fast enough. The boy who'd been condemned as a failure by his headmaster was the most eager and conscientious apprentice ever and when he was just eighteen his efforts were rewarded. Mr Weston appointed him as Relief Manager. It was a proud moment for Robert. The operation on his tongue and his devotion to the self-imposed undertaking of copying out the Bible had transformed his life. He could speak now and read but this was only the beginning. Robert was desperate to learn more and make even greater progress. He was a natural and the changes he introduced such as pre-slicing bacon and cheese saved time and pushed the sales up.

Another three years passed. Robert became the most successful Relief Manager in 'George Masons'. Wherever he was sent he found out what products the customers in that locality wanted most and then put them on special offer. He stayed late on Saturdays preparing the shop for Monday and arranging fresh, eye-catching displays. Robert loved his work and gained great satisfaction from doing a job well but deep down he was disappointed. He felt he deserved to be promoted to manage his own store but instead he was the one who was always chosen to act as a Relief Manager. Robert's expectations of himself and for his future had grown with his self-confidence, knowledge and communication skills. He didn't know what life held for him but the old miserable

existence he'd suffered right up into his mid teens
had been replaced by a life full of purpose and promise
whose boundaries were ever expanding with possib-
ilities he could never have dreamt of.

*It took courage to walk into that little chapel on my
own and sit amongst strangers.*

As Robert continued to copy out the Bible and to
think about what he read he felt a compulsion to go
to church. He chose a small church, which was only
a ten-minute walk from 335. It was a simple, basic
place, no more than a corrugated iron hut with a
wooden floor and furnished with a few rows of chairs.
Robert, who rarely went anywhere other than home
and work, walked on his own to a church he was
unfamiliar with and put himself amongst people he
did not know. It took a certain kind of courage and
proved how far he had progressed since the operation.
The members of the congregation were surprised
when this young man joined them. He had no church
background yet he knew the Bible better than many
of them. At the end of one of the services Mr Barnwell,
one of the church leaders, asked Robert directly if he
had received Jesus Christ as his Saviour. Robert had
by this time copied out John's gospel and the words
'born again' but they held no great significance for
him. He thought for a moment then answered Mr
Barnwell truthfully. He had not accepted Christ as
his Saviour. Robert was conscious of how much Mr
Barnwell wanted him to become a Christian. When
Mr Barnwell asked him if he would like to say a
prayer stating he was sorry for all he'd done wrong
and inviting Jesus into his life he did so willingly

because he respected the church leader and his sincerity and wanted to please him. The congregation welcomed Robert wholeheartedly into their fellowship. He basked in the warmth of their genuine affection and when they invited him to tea and to Sunday lunch he felt comfortable enough with them to accept. The practical expression of the love and care they felt for Robert backed up everything he learnt about the Christian faith in services and Bible studies.

Robert was coming out of his shell and enjoying interacting with others. Life had improved immeasurably for him but although he was no longer trapped in his own solitary world, he still experienced many bleak times. He could not come to terms with the fact that he had been unwanted and unloved for nearly all of his life. He worried about how it had affected his character and his capacity for loving others. Lying in his cold bed one night these thoughts kept him awake. It was past midnight and the darkness emphasized his feeling of being completely isolated, helpless and unable to face all the obstacles that lay ahead. Tears trickled down his cheeks. But amongst his unhappy random thoughts the words of John 3:16 kept running through his head. Finally Robert slid out of bed and knelt on the bare boards. He said a prayer he'd said once before with Mr Barnwell but this time he meant it with all his heart. He asked Jesus to come into his life, to forgive him for whatever he had done wrong in the past and to make him aware of God's love for him. I was free at last.

What a transformation had taken place. The boy who had believed he was worthless was a success. The teenager who had lived in fear and isolation was no longer afraid or alone but was an accepted and valued part of a community at work and at church. The person who was convinced he was unloved and uncared for had discovered how much God loved and cared for him. The Bible had freed Robert. It had liberated him from all the ills of his childhood sweeping away the bitterness and negativity that had surrounded those years. It had educated him and given him standards and principles to live by. It had led him to become a true disciple of Jesus Christ and to delight in the fact that his life was no longer hollow and empty but full of purpose and promise. It did not happen immediately, but gradually Robert did come to know God's presence in his life. His confidence grew stronger and at last he was given a shop of his own to manage in Selly Oak – the very shop where he had started as an errand boy. Nothing ever ran smoothly for Robert though. 'George Mason' was opening another shop not far away and the intention was to close the one at Selly Oak where Robert was the newly appointed manager once the new store was fitted out. Having become a manager at last Robert was determined to ensure that the Selly Oak shop stayed up and running. He put his mind to the task and with careful planning and sheer hard work increased the turnover by 300%. In fact the shop became so profitable that it continued to trade for another twenty years.

Robert had made his mark and before long he was headhunted by a new retailer. He left George Masons

and joined Tesco, a company that was taking the retail trade by storm. He started his career with Tesco as a manager and was soon promoted to regional director. People recognized Robert's qualities and he was astute enough to know where his strengths lay. Before long he left Tesco to become marketing director for the Co-operative Society and was chosen to open the first out-of-town hypermarket.

Robert's career had taken off but so had his personal life. If Robert hadn't chosen to copy out the Bible he might not have had the desire and impetus to join a church and to meet people there who cared for him and supported him. He was still working for George Mason when he was offered lodgings with one of the families from church. Robert moved out of 335 with a huge sense of relief and over the next few years and until he got married at the age of twenty-one, he made his home with Christian friends. One such family was the Ainslies. They invited Robert to share their home and to go on holiday with them. Robert revelled in the new experience of being accepted, cared about and best of all, wanted by others but even better was in store for him.

Amazingly Joyce had fallen in love with me, a love which never diminished.

One summer the Ainslies asked Robert if he would like to visit Scotland with them. Robert jumped at the chance and it was at the Guest House where they stayed that he met a seventeen-year-old girl, Joyce. She was attractive and intelligent and Robert

fell in love with her almost at first sight. He found it much harder to believe that she felt the same about him. Joyce was only young but she knew her own mind and when she was eighteen they married.

During the first seven years of their marriage Robert and Joyce were blessed with two sons, Andrew and Peter and two daughters, Julia and Joanna. These were busy years for the young couple. Robert was making a name for himself at work and Joyce had her hands full with the children, other family members and friends. Despite all the calls on her time she was constantly supportive of Robert and never complained although his work demanded that they move house seven times from one part of the country to another.

Robert received recognition nationally for his contribution to retailing but at the heart of everything he did was the Bible. He had finished copying it out some years ago but his love for the Bible and for books in general led him to change course completely. He was tired of retailing and wanted to teach and to preach the Bible. He couldn't stop thinking about it. He'd led meetings and spoken at many local church services and he was convinced that this was where his future lay. When he talked it over with the elders of his church he was so excited that he could hardly contain himself. When he'd finished they quietly told him that they were happy to recommend him to other churches as a Bible teacher but warned him that it would take a long time before he built up a full diary of appointments. Meanwhile – they had seen an advertisement for a job with the publishing arm of Scripture Union, which they believed he

should apply for even if it was only temporary.
Robert came up with all the reasons he could think
of not to go for the post of marketing manager with
SU from knowing nothing about publishing to not
being able to spell. Nevertheless with the advice of
the elders ringing in his ears he decided to apply and
give the organisation six months if he was appointed.

Scripture Union publishing was losing £1000 a week.
It was a desperate situation which severely affected
the work of this Christian movement. Robert was
offered the opportunity to turn it round. To accept
was a huge and daring step to take. He had to give
up a lucrative career, take a seventy per cent drop in
salary, move from the Wirral to London and attempt
to use his experience in selling food to selling books!
Publishing was an entirely unknown world for him.
Was this what copying out the Bible was leading him
to – the opportunity to open up the Bible to Christians
and non-Christians alike, to adults and children in
the UK and across the world? What would the teen-
aged Robert have thought as he hunched up over his
old Bible and wad of computer paper if he could have
looked to the future and seen the adult Robert hard
at work developing a new range of publishing progra-
mmes for Scripture Union?

Robert was a breath of fresh air for SU Publishing.
He brought with him new ideas, a different approach
and a keen appreciation of what the customer really
wanted. He changed the design of the publications,
introduced colour and put the prices up! He added
value by putting books into presentation cases and
these gift sets leapt off the shelves wherever they

were stocked. Then he turned his attention to Scripture Union's own chain of bookshops making them more attractive and competitive and organizing three weekly promotions which included window and counter displays. All these changes made good business sense but implementing them was not easy. Many members of the editorial, production and bookshop staff had been working in the same way for years and they were resistant to change. There was a lack of a sales mentality for there was a perception that they were missionaries rather than professionals in the publishing business. And yet Robert's motivation was no different from theirs. He wanted above all to get Bible based books into people's homes.

As time went on Robert realized that he could not change everything overnight. He could see a wonderful future for SU Publishing. He had a vision in which the movement became a major force specializing in Christian literature, Bible teaching and books for people who wanted to find out more about Jesus Christ but he had to accept that it would take years and years for his vision to become reality. Robert knew he was too impatient to wait that long but while he was part of the work force he put his heart and soul into making improvements and making money for SU. At the end of his first full year Robert turned in a profit that was greater than the total turnover for Scripture Union publishing for the previous year.

Although he had joined SU on a temporary basis Robert spent more than five years there. During that time he found a new way of making the Bible accessible

71

to children and adults. He joined forces with Ladybird, a well-known publisher of educational children's books, to produce The Ladybird Bible. It was published in twenty-four short books and Robert persuaded Yorkshire Television to run a series based on the books. It was called God's Story and was screened at Easter and Christmas and repeated some three years later. Both the book and the TV series were a great success. The Ladybird Bible was a children's bestseller for ten consecutive years. Hundreds of thousands of children and their parents were introduced to the Bible and when Robert persuaded an American publisher to become involved in a co-edition, the project grew even larger.

My life's work wasn't the itinerant Bible teaching I had expected. In some ways it was bigger and potentially more influential.

Despite all he had brought to SU and all he had accomplished with the movement, Robert knew he had to leave. Too many people could not accept his commercial outlook. It was alien to them and the whole set up hampered the publishing arm in its efforts to become a mainstream business. But the frustrations Robert encountered in his daily work did not make leaving any easier. Making the decision to go was painful especially as his experience with SU had shown him that his future lay in making Bible material attractive and accessible to all. Robert had been convinced that he should become an itinerant preacher but after his time with SU he knew for sure that he had found his life's work.

Although he was out of a job, he wasn't worried. He was excited, bubbling over with ideas and he couldn't wait to use all he had learned at SU to help others publish top quality Bible based products. He established a company, Creative Publishing, not intending to publish anything himself but to encourage others and bring about innovations in the marketing of Christian books. Robert threw himself into his new calling but he hit a brick wall. Nobody wanted to take his ideas on board. They were not interested in his packaging suggestions and spurned his advice on the need to use colour. Too many companies and organisations were satisfied with a customer base that consisted of committed Christians who regularly bought their products. Robert wanted to reach out to people who didn't normally buy such books. He knew such people would need to be attracted by colourful, professionally produced Bibles, Gospels and Bible reading notes if they were to be persuaded to purchase them. In the end Robert realized he would have to show others how to do it. He had no idea at the time that over the years to come his company would publish some sixty million pieces mostly distributed through organizations and churches. 'Personalized' Gospels were a big hit. The Gospels were produced with a specially printed cover and given away at special events. When Billy Graham came to Britain in 1984 and 1985 Robert produced colour magazines for the missions and offered them a hundred thousand copies of Luke's Gospel free of charge. Creative Publishing's colour New Testament was taken by the Germans and given out to East Germans when the Berlin wall came down. By collaborating with overseas publishers Robert's company was responsible for hundreds of

thousands of co-editions of scriptural verses and devotional books. Some projects didn't work but many were huge successes but for Robert success wasn't measured in commercial terms but in the impact the books had on people's lives.

Running his own business meant Robert scarcely had a moment to himself but the constant demands Creative Publishing made on his time and energy never drained him. Full of enthusiasm, optimism and new ideas Robert travelled throughout the UK and abroad in pursuit of his mission to produce Christian literature. Sometimes the travelling was in vain and he would come home without the contract he'd worked so hard to win but any disappointment and tiredness would be put aside as he planned what he could do to remedy the situation. It was after one of these unsuccessful trips to America that Robert landed at Heathrow where Joyce was waiting to drive him home. Robert was delighted to be reunited with his wife. He settled himself in the car and allowed himself the luxury of thinking ahead, imagining getting home, eating a meal, having a bath and falling into bed. Joyce spoke, breaking into his pleasant reverie. What she said, quietly and casually, shocked Robert to the core. His mother had been found. At first Robert didn't believe Joyce. Later the tears flowed freely as the pent up emotions, which had been pushed to the back of his mind for over twenty years, overwhelmed him. Robert had never tried to trace his mother. He had done his best to blot out the past and to forge a new life for himself. He did not want to dwell on the pain and bitterness of his childhood. Instead every day he consciously

appreciated the love of his wife and children, the satisfaction he felt as a result of making something of himself and the fulfilment he gained from his work, which he regarded as a ministry. But within two hours of arriving home Robert was travelling again, this time up the motorway to pick up his mother and take her to Birmingham where she was going to stay with Jean.

Although Robert didn't really want to talk about the past his mother did. He listened patiently and so he learned about how she had made a living in the twenty seven years since she left, how ill she had been and why she hadn't started searching for her children until quarter of a century had passed when her fear of her husband finding her and dragging her back into their abusive relationship had faded.

The reunion with the rest of the family was highly charged and emotional. There was much to understand and to forgive and it was not easy. But Winifred Hicks was a very different person from the woman her children remembered. Looking back she could see where she had gone wrong and was sorry for it. She had rediscovered her faith and found consolation and healing. Winifred was also very ill. Not long after she moved into sheltered accommodation she died. Robert had given her a Bible at that first family reunion and just before she died she wrote: 'In times of problems I know I can turn to Jesus, for I know I have been forgiven.'

Another chapter of my life had closed. Old wounds had been opened and had healed. But new wounds were to occur which I had never expected.

The years flew by. Peter went to university in Bath. Robert and Joyce took a liking to the city and decided to move there. At the time Andrew was working as a football coach in the USA, Julia was planning to get married in Bath and Jo was able to move schools without disrupting her education. The family settled happily in Bath and soon made many friends as well as being visited regularly by colleagues in the business of Christian publishing. These were frantically busy years and before they knew it Robert and Joyce were approaching their silver wedding anniversary. Despite all the ups and downs of married life they were enjoying their time together to the full. They shared so many memories and with Julia's wedding fixed for September, the same month as their anniversary, there seemed to be everything to look forward to and be grateful for. But a terrible blow awaited them.

It was a grey, cold, wet January day when Robert and Joyce drove to their local hospital. After a short wait they were called into a small room off an anonymous corridor. They faced a consultant across a desk, which was heaped with folders and bits of paper. The consultant was elderly with years of experience behind him. He broke the news as gently as he could but what he said was devastating.

81

My beautiful wife, Joyce, had cancer.

Joyce had a fast growing cancer. It had already spread to her lymph system. She had had a mole removed from her leg some sixteen years before. Although it was malignant the surgeon was certain that it had all been removed and no more was said. Now it appeared Joyce had been carrying the disease in her body all this time despite the surgeon's optimistic statement. Somehow Robert managed to detach his emotions long enough for him to question the consultant closely. There was not a vestige of hope in any one of his answers. He thought Joyce had about six months left to live.

One minute life is normal, the past understood and the future predictable, the next it has fallen apart. Everyone and everything else continued as normal but for Robert and Joyce there was no normality, just shock and disbelief. Only by going over and over what had been said in the consulting room did they begin to come to terms with what they had been told. Joyce had a form of cancer that was incurable and had only a short time to live.

All the information I received was painful.

The pressures in those early days were intolerable. Children and parents had to be told and comforted. Meanwhile, Joyce had convinced herself that Robert was the one person capable of finding a cure for her illness. Humbled by the faith his wife had in him, Robert felt paralysed by the helplessness that came

from the knowledge that this was a challenge that was beyond him. Nevertheless, both he and Joyce investigated every avenue they could think of. Joyce looked into alternative and complimentary medicine while Robert explored the more orthodox treatments. The prognosis was not good and as they were searching feverishly for answers Joyce collapsed and was rushed hospital. She had hepatitis.

We began to live a rich, full life, being involved in the lives of many other people.

Once back home again Joyce started on a special diet to which she stuck rigidly. Her faith gave her peace of mind. She was not afraid of what lay ahead and she was conscious of being safe in God's hands. Being Joyce, she soon began to make plans to help other people diagnosed with cancer. She took over an apartment that belonged to Robert's company and welcomed other cancer sufferers to come and stay. Despite her debilitating illness Joyce gave herself to others and even organised a conference week attended by fifty people. She began arranging dried flowers to raise money to support those struck down by the disease. As for herself, she was in constant pain and unable to take painkillers because of the diet she so strictly adhered to.

85

True friends rallied round. There were flowers, cards, letters, visits and prayers to help Joyce through the eight operations and the removal of forty tumours. The love and comfort Joyce received made both her and Robert feel privileged and special and, to their delight, they became grandparents.

But as the illness took its toll Joyce became steadily weaker day by day. Robert was her rock. Caring for his wife filled his days and yet as time went on he experienced something quite unexpected – he fell in love with Joyce all over again. It was very hard for Robert though. Joyce's special diet kept her housebound and whenever Robert left the house he felt guilty. He had to remain positive for Joyce but in his heart he was already grieving for her.

Joyce fought cancer bravely for two and a half years. She was not afraid of dying, convinced that God knew what he was doing. Facing death had made her and Robert appreciate one another more than ever and they both realized that what really mattered was not what they had but who they were. They read the Bible together and Robert began selecting and paraphrasing passages, which were particularly meaningful to them both.

87

So the unwelcome guest came. Joyce reached out, took him by the hand and left her loving family in God's strong hands.

When the time came Joyce entrusted her family to Robert and them all to God's loving protection while she slipped away to a place where there was no pain or suffering and where her faith and love would be rewarded.

Robert organized a thanksgiving service for Joyce. Over two hundred people came and ten close friends spoke of her faith, love, hope and generosity of spirit. Afterwards Robert struggled with his loss. He felt

cheated and afraid, lonely and angry but above all bereft. Joyce had been his constant companion. She had taught him that love was real and that life was full of opportunities, adventure and meaning.

Alone in an empty house Robert dwelt on the last few hours he and Joyce had spent together. He recalled how she had looked into the darkness of death and had seen the light and love of God. Robert resolved that he would face the darkness of his tomorrows and seek that same light and love.

Take away my worldly goods – but I will still serve you.

Only weeks after Joyce's death Robert's faith and hope was tested yet again. Before Joyce had fallen ill she and Robert had been to see a property another couple had bought, done up and were selling on for a good profit. They were impressed and the husband asked Robert if he would like to join him in setting up a company specializing in property development. Robert agreed to take a 45% stake in the company but said he would have to be a sleeping partner as he had too many other commitments. He guaranteed a hundred thousand pound loan from the bank for a year and he put his own property, which he was renovating, into the company. But when interest rates shot up it became impossible to sell the properties the company had bought unless it was at a huge loss. Then a few weeks after Joyce died the bank called in their loan. At a time when he was struggling to come to terms with his bereavement Robert had to cope with huge financial demands, the possibility of losing his home and the breakdown of his relationship with

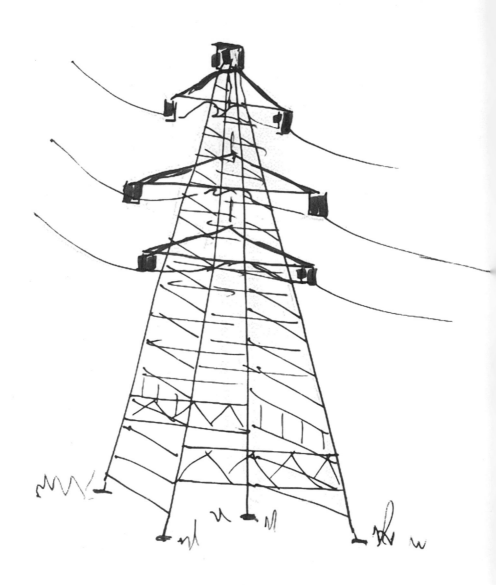

his business partner. It was almost too much to bear. But worse was to follow. The bank seized the assets of Creative Publishing even though they had no right to do so. To lose the love of his life after thirty months of desperately trying to find a way to conquer her illness was devastating yet on top of this Robert had to face the ongoing nightmare of dealing with an organisation that treated him clinically and unfairly. But Robert didn't go under. His faith remained unshaken. He took on the bank single handedly and spent months sorting out the whole sorry mess. Robert honoured his partnership agreement paying both his and his partner's share of the losses. He was determined that he wouldn't allow these setbacks to dominate his life. Instead he used this frightening and bitter experience as a learning opportunity. His two sons and their families depended on the publishing business for their livelihood and Robert wanted them to be secure. They needed to do something else to generate capital so he, Peter and Andrew set up a new company, Robert Frederick Limited, producing children's books and gift books – and they didn't borrow a penny from the bank! It was a new start for Robert in his business life and he was soon to make a new start in his personal life too.

I needed someone to love, and be loved by.

Robert had met Joyce through the Ainslie family who attended the same church as him and once again it was Mrs Ainslie who was instrumental in his meeting Annabelle. A few months later, in 1991, Robert and Annabelle married and three years on they were blessed with a daughter, Emily-Rose.

Despite the passing years Robert remained full of life, enthusiasm and ideas. As the millennium approached he worked flat out to use this momentous time to spread God's word across the nation. He organised and sponsored 'The Perfect Way to Commemorate the Millennium' with The Daily Telegraph and made a similar arrangement with The Daily Express called 'The Perfect Start'. Through these two national newspapers Robert gave away millions of copies of a Millennium gospel which he had had printed with a special commemorative cover. It was an amazingly simple but effective way of getting a copy of St Luke's gospel into homes all over Britain and the editor of The Daily Telegraph acknowledged that it was one of the most successful joint ventures his paper had been involved in.

93

Always looking forward Robert envisaged producing gospels for people in countries across the world. His new non-profit making venture was to print gospels in places such as India, China and Russia and he set himself a target of one billion copies over the first decade of the new millennium. With each of his new projects Robert was keeping a promise he'd made in the mid 1950's.

Robert was about fifteen and had not yet had the operation on his tongue when he met the Wise family at the little Jiggins Lane Gospel Hall. Mr and Mrs Wise and their young daughter befriended Robert. and most Sundays they invited him to share lunch with them. Fred Wise worried about Robert, not just that the boy had so many problems and never had enough to eat but also that he always wore old, ill-

fitting clothes for he had no other choice. One day, before taking his wife and daughter off on their annual holiday Fred Wise who was a bread deliveryman and not well-off sold his green-house and from the proceeds gave Robert ten shillings. He asked him to use the money to buy a shirt, a pair of trousers and a pair of shoes. Robert was embarrassed. His pride was hurt. Fred's kind generosity brought home to him what other people must think when they saw him dressed like a lad who was living rough. He mumbled his thanks but made a vow to God that sometime in the future he would return that ten shillings thousands upon thousands of times over to others. A Service of Thanksgiving was held for Fred after he died in 1999. The person who conducted the service knew both Fred and Robert and he related the story of the ten-shilling gift to the teenager who had difficulty in speaking and could hardly read or write. It was a gift of love to a youngster who appeared to have no prospects but that same youngster grew into the man who was the driving force behind the Millennium Gospel project ensuring that schools, churches and tens of thousands of individuals received copies of the good news of Jesus Christ.

In 2002 Robert had a very special Bible to give away. Towards the end of the Queen's Golden Jubilee year, he, Annabelle and Emily-Rose made a trip to Buckingham Palace to present a new copy of the King James' Bible which Robert and a friend had had redesigned and re-typeset. It was a wonderful and joyful occasion for a man who some forty-five years before had laboriously copied out by hand this same 350-year-old translation of God's word.

Conclusion

Comments from Alan Bain, BBC Producer & Presenter:
This was a sad, depressing house to film; heartbreaking.
Being myself a Londoner who has viewed human life
at its most raw, I have become accustomed to the
difficult parts of life, but I do not know how Robert
survived all this and at the same time struggled being
tongue-tied and dyslexic. If I had not witnessed the
filming that day, I would have found his story difficult
to believe, and even more difficult to enter into his
experiences.

There was one room that Robert did not enter; that
was his father's bedroom – "A dark room of bad
memories" is how he described it. Still the fear and
horror of that place reached from the young child
across the years to the adult man, and prevented
him from entering.

Following the home filming, we eventually moved on
to the Institution which had been "Middlemore Homes"
and part of Robert's childhood. The premises are now
part of Birmingham University and the then Principal
had given permission for the filming. As he showed
us round, I learned that – a few weeks earlier – Robert
had enjoyed a private meal with the Principal just a
stone's throw from the spot where, fifty years earlier,
as a deprived bruised and battered boy he had arrived

at the Institution and had 'breakfasted' at suppertime on curled-up sandwiches.

Then his clothes had been removed, his hair shaved and he had been disinfected in the shower before sleeping in a huge dormitory of army-style beds between white starched sheets. We filmed inside that dormitory. Where there had once been twenty-two beds for boys, now there are twenty-two computers occupying students from round the world. What a contrast!

Over the past dozen years, I have grown to know Robert. I remember, when he first came into publishing, how he revolutionised a lot of thinking because of his professional marketing approach. I am constantly amazed at the wide range of enterprises he initiates, sponsors and encourages.

However, after the filming at 335 Stonehouse Lane, I realise I am just beginning to understand the man himself.

ALAN BAIN, Friend and BBC Bristol Producer & Presenter 1998-2001.

As I look back over the years, I can see the gracious hand of a good and loving God guiding a flawed personality through all the changing scenes of life, in trouble and in joy. To him above all I am deeply thankful.

A Child's Thoughts

When I recollected some of my thinking as a child, which I have scattered through-out my previous book "A Child Cries", a few kind friends informed me that these "thoughts" had a power of their own, in their raw state and without comment.

THOUGHT PATTERNS WITHOUT WORDS

My only comment therefore, by way of introduction to "A Child's Thoughts" is to say that, because communicating verbally was nearly impossible except for immediate family and a few friends who had learned to understand my peculiar way of speaking, I did spend countless hours every day thinking and reasoning within myself. Indeed, I held conversations with imaginary individuals, or imaginary conversations with real people. This, coupled with the developing powers of observation - that all children are blessed with – is the reason why I have no difficulty in remembering those "Child's Thoughts".

Of course, the adult now in me has occasionally added to the vocabulary, but, looking back, I realise that I did have quite an extensive vocabulary even though I could not read, write or speak, as I should. I do hope this section of the book will open up your own emotions to the needs of present day children near and far.

1

"No-one can see my tears because they are inside, deep inside, and they hurt."

2

The Slums, the children's homes. Now 'home'. All strange places to live. I wonder what next.

3

"One day, I will be free...! One day, I will be someone...!"

4

"Slumland was a place where a lot of small minded people lived small small lives, but not much smaller than most people outside of slumland. Funny that and a bit sad really."

5

"All I am to my Mum and Dad is an allowance from the Government and a ration book for food, not their son."

6

"The way for me to overcome not being able to read is page by page and word by word even if it takes years to do it"

7

"I am a stranger at home and an idiot at school,
a wild boy outside."

8

"Maybe, one day, I will have someone to help me.
Maybe, one day, I will have a friend... but I am not
sure. Maybe's are only dreams."

9

"My head is full, my heart is heavy, my speech is
wrong, my home is cold, my life is empty. That's me
in a nutshell."

10

"What do I want...? ...to be able to talk, to be able
to read, to be able to write, to be able to belong, to
be able to laugh and to be happy on the inside."

11

"All my life, I have been robbed. But no more."

12

"They do not understand what I am saying. I cannot
say what they want me to. I am not the same as
other children. If only I could speak the way they
want me to!"

13

"I don't like the kitchen at night. It is the worst place in all the world. It is cold and I am all alone with Dad. I am afraid."

14

"They told me I had a home to go to, but they did not tell me about the kitchen or the bedrooms or my Mom or my Dad."

15

"I think I should me happy. Something must be wrong"

16

"I was born in a bombing raid, neglected in the slums, taken into care with no voice to speak..... not much to start life with!"

17

"I was her fourth child but she never knew my birthday. She never knew me - not even for one day in a year."

18

"I don't remember when I was very little but I know I was never allowed to be 'myself'. I was alone and unloved."

19

"I was told I had a baby sister, but I have never seen
her. I want to see her and in a strange way
I miss her very much."

20

"The men sing loud songs and smell of beer, and
then they are sick and the buckets come out week
after week."

21

"Jesus had a manger, I had a cardboard box.
I am glad Jesus wasn't born in a palace."

22

"My first awareness came more in impressions than
thoughts; impressions of an unhappy start in life.
My nostrils rebelled against the vile smells.
My ears closed to the excessively loud noises.
My eyes constantly looked away.
My taste spoiled by grease and lard.
My flesh jerked away from the slightest touch. It
was as though all my senses were at war with their
environment, with no protection from Mother or
Father."

23

"I like it here. It's warm and there's hot food and
children to play with and a big woman who smiles.
But I know it won't last."

24

"They offered me a home: they gave me Hell."

25

"Mom has lots of children, but not lots of love. Maybe no love at all."

26

"Can she be my mother? Is this my real mother who will love me, talk to me, listen to me and care for me? No: I don't think she really is my mother!"

27

"I don't know who I am, why I am here or how long I will stay here, but I know it's better than where I was before. That was horrible. They tell me I can stay for Christmas. I don't know what Christmas is.
They tell me I will have hot food and lots of presents, but I don't believe them. I know somebody will take me away. I wish I could stop for Christmas and have hot food and lots of presents."

28

"Today, I walked a long way from the warm Home to a cold house and it was very, very cold."

29

"I don't like it when it's quiet. Bad things can happen in the quiet."

30

"I cannot understand why Mom has taken me away from a warm house and hot food and children to play with and Christmas. I feel so cold and hungry and I don't think Christmas is going to come to our house."

31

"What is a friend? It must be someone who does not expect to gain anything from you, but wants to be with you whenever he can. Maybe no-one in the world has a real friend. I don't think I will ever have a real friend. I wonder if I could be a real friend to somebody. One day, I will try."

32

"My sister has a room all to herself. I wish I had a room to myself, then I could have a bed to myself instead of sharing it with all my brothers."

33

"They work all the time on their garden. It's as though it is all they have in the whole world … their garden. There must be something special about a garden."

34

"I miss my shiny pennies! I miss my bar of chocolate! I miss my game of hoop-la! I miss them all. They were given to me. I had not been given things before."

35

"Other children in the Lane have told me they get cards and presents for their birthdays. Only John and Jean have got presents in our house. Bernard, Brian and I do not. I wonder why we never get cards or presents. Mom and Dad spend their money when they go out every night. Maybe that's the reason why."

36

"I remember the slums; the smells, the noises and the children. I wish they could all come out into the countryside. Bartley Green is big enough for everyone!"

37

"I went a long walk to where the children play on swings while their mothers talk to each other. The mothers looked so happy talking and they never seemed to stop. The children looked so happy playing and they never seemed to stop either. I am glad that some families have nice mothers and children.I wish Dad and Mom would come to the playground and see how happy people can be."

38

"I know how to count the stars in the sky! I make a circle with my first finger and thumb and stretch it from my eye until I can count a hundred stars. Then I move the circle around the sky and count how many circles it needs to cover the sky. There are hundreds of hundreds of stars!"

39
"I lived in two places at the same time, but they were not the same."

40
"I know people think I am crazy because I talk to myself, but if I don't do it, I will never learn to speak."

41
"I keep humming quietly to myself. I don't know why, but the vibration from the humming stops the pain from thoughts I cannot share with anyone. I like thinking, but I wish I could talk as well."

42
"I can't understand it! I want to be happy in my new home with all the family, but I don't want to come home until it is dark, because then I can crawl into bed without Mom or Dad knowing. I don't think they miss me anyway. I don't understand it."

43
"The brook is clean, fresh and flowing, and when the sun is out it is warm. I don't hum when I can hear the sound of the brook. Over and over it says, "Tickle, tickle…" I put my feet into the water and it tickles me. The birds and I like coming to the brook. It keeps us happy."

44

"The worm doesn't like coming out of the ground because it is dangerous. The birds might eat it. I like getting out of the house because it is safer outside. The worm stops in the dark, afraid to come into the light. I stay as long as I can in the light, afraid of going back into the dark house. I am glad I am not a worm, but I wish I was not afraid of the night at home."

45

"The Lane is full of children. I am so glad this is not the slums."

46

"I like the buttercup and daisy flowers in the fields. They both have bright yellow eyes looking up, but they close at night time. I feel like the field flowers. When I am out of the house something inside me opens up as I walk the fields talking to myself. When I get home at night, something inside me closes down and all I can do is hum quietly to myself."

47

"Mom and Dad don't notice me. Jean never speaks to me; Donald and John do sometimes. Bernard and Brian talk to each other. I speak but no-one listens. Most of the time, I talk to myself in my head. I think I must live inside my head. I wish I could get my thoughts out of my head."

48

"I dreamed again of the red robin who I trapped in a cage. I now understand why he kept hurting himself trying to escape from the trap. I now understand why when he escaped, he never came back.
One day, I will escape! One day, I will be free!"

49

"I like it when Dad tells us the stories of the war, but I can't believe that everyone else is bad but us."

50

"The farmer's black and white horses are strong, very strong - much stronger than the farmer. Yet they do everything the farmer tells them to do. The farmer looks very small by the side of the horses, but they never run away from him, no matter how hard they work or tired they become. I wonder what the secret of the farmer is?"

51

"It's strange to think that in our small village of Bartley Green we had the tallest lady in the world. I wonder where the tallest man is!"

52

"I missed the Sunday hot food today. I must go to school tomorrow, or I will die without food."

53

"There was a nice song at the Children's Club at the little 'tin hut' church: "What can I give Him, poor as I am? If I were a shepherd, I would bring a lamb. If I were a wise man, I would do my part, Yet what can I give Him? Give my heart!"

54

"The stars have been there from the beginning which means I can see the same stars as anybody else. This makes me the same as everybody else. I am glad!"

55

"I dreamed today that I was a good boy and that everybody wanted to talk and to listen to me. I dreamed I was living in a big house with a big kitchen with lots of hot food. I know it was only a dream, but I liked it very much. Maybe, one day, the dream will come true! But I'm not sure."

56

"What a greater fool I have been, to have spent so long looking in the gutter, when I could have been enjoying God's creation all around me!"

57

"I wish people would smile like Miss Treadwell. When she smiles at me, I am happy. When I am happy, I can smile too. When I smile at Mrs. Taylor next door, she smiles back. If Mom and Dad could

smile, maybe they would be happy. I smile at them, but most times I don't think they notice me. One time, Dad said, "What are you grinning at?" as if I should not be smiling."

58
"I like my teacher, Miss Treadwell. She doesn't talk to me as there are too many of us in the classroom, but she does notice me. When she looks at me, she smiles at me. Mom never looks at me or smiles. I wish Miss Treadwell was my Mom, but I don't think she would like my Dad."

59
"I don't like taking my 'Free Dinner' tickets to my teacher at school. The tickets tell everyone that my Mom and Dad don't look after me. I don't like the other children knowing I have free meals. They say nasty things and tease me. But I do like the food. I know I must eat plenty at school as there is no food at home. I don't want to starve to death!"

60
"The puddings we have at school are tapioca, semolina or sponge with custard. I don't like the tapioca – it reminds me of frogs spawn. The semolina is slimy. I do like the sponge with the hot custard. I eat all the puddings, even the ones I don't like because I know there will be nothing to eat at home in the evening."

61

"I like John a lot, but I am also jealous because he can speak right and play the piano and everybody likes him. I wish somebody would like me."

62

"We had a big bonfire in front of our house for 'Guy Fawkes Night'. I was pleased because I collected most of the wood for burning, walking many miles to find broken branches. The neighbours like the big fire and cooked their potatoes at the edge of it. They gave me some potatoes and they tasted so good! Some children had 'sparklers'. I wish I had a sparkler."

63

"I don't like the five of us sleeping in the same bed. I wish I had my own bed, like in the Children's Homes. Donald keeps most of the coat to himself and John keeps making wheezing noises. I was wet again this morning and I don't want to keep sleeping in this bed next to my brother who can't help wetting it. I wish I had my own bed!"

64

"We have everything. We have nothing. It's scary."

65

"The teacher keeps telling me to get my hair cut. I keep telling my Mom, but she never listens.

When a letter came from the teacher, Mom put a basin over my head and cut my hair around it using her own spittle to control the hair. Now I know why they call it a 'basin cut'. My hair feels funny so short. It won't be cut again for a long time."

66

"I went to the 'Saturday Matinee' for the first time today and was surprised to see how many children were there. The picture house was full! The children sang lots of songs I had never heard before. "Hop Along Cassidy" was the hero of the film and he could always outshoot the bad men, even when riding fast on his horse. I hope I will become a cowboy one day."

67

"The 'Pictures' fill my mind with so many ideas and help me forget home. I know it's not real. The films are like my dreams, but I like them. Maybe, one day, I will have a horse. Maybe, one day, I will ride away and go anywhere I want to. Maybe, one day, I will be somebody."

68

"Jean looks funny. Bernard looks funny. Brian speaks funny. I speak funny. But it's not funny. It's not fair. Why can't we just be normal the same as everyone else?"

69

"Tiger, the cat, had kittens in my bed in the night. She came to me because I am her friend and I hum and she purrs to me. Dad drowned all the kittens in the morning because we have no food for them. I keep crying in my heart. Only Tiger hears me. She looks so sad and has stopped purring and now cries in 'miaows' for her lost kittens. Dad has told me I must not let Tiger come in the house again – but I will."

70

"I wish I could stop dreaming of running around looking for food and only wearing a short shirt. I wish Dad and Mom were not always in my dreams eating my food. I don't like night time."

71

"I am good at Maths in school. I am always at the top of the class. The teacher said I am good enough to be top of the school. I can 'see' the answers without a lot of thinking. Is it because I am thinking all the time? I like Maths, but I wish I could read as well. I can work out numbers easily, but I cannot understand alphabet letters. I do not understand why."

72

"Why can I not speak what is in my mind? When the teacher speaks, I understand. When he

*gives me books to read and write in, I don't.
I wish he would speak more and not give me the
books, but I do like looking at the pictures in them."*

73

*"I am late again for school. Dad made me go up
Jiggins Lane to get his newspaper first. The paper
is called "The Mirror". The first time I went for it,
I thought I was getting a new mirror for the wall
to replace the cracked one Dad uses for shaving.
The man at the shop insisted that Dad wanted the
newspaper. He was right. Dad did not tell me off for
bringing a newspaper instead of a mirror, but they
caned me at school for being late."*

74

*"Mr. Woolley wanted to cane me today. He said
I had cheated at Maths. I refused to be caned.
Mr. Woolley became red in the face. I felt sorry for
Mr. Woolley, but it would not be fair for me to be
punished for something I did not do. I am always
being punished for nothing."*

75

*"The old oak tree is full of mystery and secrets. It's
heart is big enough for three of us and I like to hide
inside it or climb up into its branches and see a long
way off."*

76

"Today, I pulled some of the farmer's carrots out of the ground to eat. I put the green tops back into the soil but I don't think they will grow again. I hope he won't mind me having the carrots, as I am so hungry."

77

"I love the fresh water from the spring that started running when the world began. I feel so clean inside when I drink it."

78

"I stole a pack of playing cards, but I don't like playing with them. It was wrong. I wish I could take them back. I am sorry for the lonely man who may not have money to buy some more."

79

"New clothes for just one day! I am not surprised to lose them. The big surprise was to have them at all."

80

"I wanted to feel special having time alone with my Mom for a day's outing. But now the day has come, I don't feel special. She doesn't want to talk to me. She wants to talk to a strange man."

81

"I saw Mom kiss and cuddle a tall black man on the coach coming back from her Works' Outing. I know

Mom will leave us one day. She doesn't love Dad or us. She only wanted me with her on the outing so that Dad would not know she was with this man. I saw so many people happy today, including my Mom. I am not happy."

82

"I am ten now but I never get new clothes to keep. One day Mom did get me new clothes that I thought were for me to keep. I wore the suit to go with Mom on her Works' Outing a long way away. I wished the trousers were long instead of short, but it didn't really matter because I only wore the suit once."

83

"Slowly, I am losing my family. It's like a slow death."

84

"Donald ran away again and now he is in trouble and we are told we will not see him for a long, long time, if ever. It's not his fault! It's Mom and Dad's fault! Why haven't we got a proper Mom and Dad? It isn't fair that I won't see Donald again."

85

"Mom has stopped cooking a dinner on Sundays and she spends most of her time back in the city. I don't know if I really miss her, but I know something terrible is going to happen."

86

"I cannot hug you, Mom. I cannot! Cannot! Cannot! I don't want to, because you don't really want to hug me or be near me or understand me. You're always saying you'll leave us and I know you will one day. But it's cold at night and we need your coat on our bed."

87

"Why did you say I did not love you, as if it was my fault? Why did you say you were leaving us all, as if it was our fault? Why did you want to say, 'Goodbye'?"

88

"Mom... I don't understand why you have run away and not taken Jean with you! Jean is now the only girl, all alone and afraid."

89

"John... I am so pleased you are my big brother. I need you. Please don't go away as well."

90

"Today I only got dry sandwiches. I was expecting hot food like I got at the other Children's Home. I hoped that nice cuddly lady would be here with her smiling face but it's a different Home. How I miss her!"

91

"My Mom has gone. My hair has gone. My clothes have gone. My family has gone. I am all alone again."

92

"I am still hungry, but now I feel clean inside and out after the shower and now this bed that smells so nice. I wonder what will happen next."

93

"I look strange in the grey clothes and they feel so heavy, but I know they are not really mine. Children at school also know they don't belong to me and they make fun of me."

94

"Today, I made friends with the leader of a 'gang'. He needs a friend. All the boys need a friend. Inside they are so empty."

95

"The boys look so sad. They look as if they are always about to cry. I wish there was someone who could help them."

96

"I played cricket today with John and some other boys. John was not happy when I 'caught him out'. When it was my turn to bat, he was not happy because he couldn't get me 'out' and I wouldn't declare.

The girls who were watching left, so in the end John and the boys left also. I was the smallest boy playing and I think I spoiled the game for them, but I am still pleased with how well I played."

97

"God! God! Why am I imprisoned in this cage so long? The robin only suffered for a short time and I let him go free as soon as I saw his distress. Why can I not be free and live a 'normal' life?"

98

"I watched a spider making its web in the bushes. Although it spends a long time making its web, I know that tomorrow it will have lots of breaks in it and the spider will start all over again. The teacher keeps telling me to try and try again to read. I do keep trying, but I can't see the words on the page. I really do want to learn to read and, like the spider, I don't mind trying again... but I just can't see the words on the page. How can other children see the words to read?" "Mom has gone - but she was never really here. How I miss her coat!"

99

"I know inside my heart I cry a lot. But no-one can see the tears. I even cry inside when I am smiling outside. I don't want them to know I have been crying. When I grow up, I will never cry again because when I am an adult no-one will be able to hurt me."

100

"I climbed right high up an electric pylon and heard the funny whirring sound of the wires. I only did it because the girls were not talking to me and I wanted them to take notice. The park keeper saw me and came running and shouting. I came down very fast and ran away. Later, he came to our house and told Dad I could easily have been electrocuted."

101

"The world is spinning round fast according to the teacher at school. I have worked out that if I jump high enough, the earth will spin beneath me and I will land in a place further on. Maybe I have found a new way of travelling! The women who live nearby look at me strangely while I test my new idea."

102

"Today I kept ten shillings that was not mine. I feel ashamed. Ten shillings is the most money I have ever had. I spent a few pennies and I really did want to take the rest back, but I knew I would be in trouble for spending the pennies. It was not worth having that money that did not belong to me. It worried me too much. I don't want to get bad like Dad."

103

"Will I ever have some chocolate again? It is such a long time since Donald stole my bar of chocolate. I wonder how much longer I will have to wait."

104

"A lady who lives near school sells toffee apples at lunch break time. I sometimes get the 'core' from other children and sometimes there's a bit of toffee apple left too. I like toffee apple. I am going to save some pennies to buy one all to myself. One day I will have a toffee apple all to myself."

105

"I never know when I come home at night which of my brothers will be missing or have been sent away again."

Table of Events

1941   Born in the slums during an air-raid.
          Born severely tongue-tied and dyslexic.

1941-5   Life in the 'slums' and Institutions

1946   Mother appears

1946-7   Worst winter of the century

1946   A first 'Christmas' anticipated

1952   Mother deserts family

1953   Middlemore Children's Homes

1953-6   Fear of Dad

1956   15th Birthday - Fight Dad for freedom

1956   Errand boy for family grocer

1956-8   Copying out The Bible by hand

1957-60   Apprenticeship to become 'Master Grocer'

1960	'Best Relief Manager' in the Company
1961	Married to Joyce
1962-9	Birth of 2 sons and 2 daughters
1968-72	From 'Manager' to 'Area Director'
1973-79	'Marketing Director' in North-West of England
1979-84	Moved to London to become Publisher
1984	Start new Company. First production 'Offer of Life' – John's Gospel
1987	Joyce diagnosed with Cancer
1989	Joyce dies
1991	Married to Annabelle
1994	Birth of daughter, Emily-Rose
1999	8 million 'Millennium Gospels'
2000	Joint promotions with 'Daily Telegraph' and 'Daily Express'
2002	Conceived 'Welcome Back to Church'
2004	Manchester Diocese initiate 'Back to Church'

2009/10   Millions of 'Fresh Retellings' of the
           Gospels

2010   Bible Companion for 'Lausanne' and
           friends

2011   Celebrations for 400 years of 'King
           James/AV' Bible which "The Boy" wrote
           out in 1956-8

*"I have always held on to a simple dream, which is that
if the Jesus of the Four Gospels could impact on my life for
good, surely the same Jesus can only do good to all who
discover Him for themselves in the same Gospel books."*

127